12/11

D1542709

WAR STORIES

PILOTS IN PERIL

Brian Williams

Heinemann
LIBRARY

Chicago, Illinois

www.heinemannraintree.com
Visit our website to find out more information about Heinemann-Raintree books.

To order:
☎ Phone 888-454-2279
💻 Visit www.heinemannraintree.com to browse our catalog and order online.

© 2012 Heinemann Library
an imprint of Capstone Global Library, LLC
Chicago, Illinois

Edited by Louise Galpine and Vaarunika Dharmapala
Designed by Clare Webber and Steve Mead
Original illustrations © Capstone Global Library
 Ltd 2011
Illustrated by KJA-Artists.com
Picture research by Elizabeth Alexander
Originated by Capstone Global Library Ltd
Printed and bound in China by Leo Paper
 Products Ltd

15 14 13 12 11
10 9 8 7 6 5 4 3 2 1

Library of Congress Cataloging-in-Publication Data
Williams, Brian, 1943–
 Pilots in peril / Brian Williams.
  p. cm.—(War stories)
 Includes bibliographical references and index.
 ISBN 978-1-4329-4830-6 (hc)—ISBN 978-1-4329-4838-2 (pb) 1. Air pilots, Military—Juvenile literature. I. Title.
 UG631.W55 2012
 358.4'14—dc22   2010029564

Acknowledgments
We would like to thank the following for permission to reproduce photographs: Alamy pp. **9** (© Mary Evans Picture Library), **12** (© RIA Novosti), **21** (© INTERFOTO), **22** (© Trinity Mirror/Mirrorpix); Corbis pp. **4** (© Bettmann), **5** (© Lee Corkran/Sygma), **15** (© Paul Bowen/Science Faction), **16–17** (© Hulton-Deutsch Collection), **24–25** (© YANNIS BEHRAKIS/Reuters), **27** (© RUBEN SPRICH/Reuters); Getty Images pp. **7** (Hulton Archive), **10** (Keystone), **13** (Popperfoto), **18** (Popperfoto), **23** (KIM JAE-HWAN/AFP); Shutterstock **background design and features** (© oriontrail).

Cover photograph of a re-creation of the Japanese attack on Pearl Harbor from the 1970 movie *Tora! Tora! Tora!*, reproduced with permission of Corbis (© Douglas Kirkland).

We would like to thank John Allen Williams, Professor of Political Science, Loyola University, Chicago, for his invaluable help in the preparation of this book.

CONTENTS

Words appearing in the text in bold, **like this**, are explained in the glossary.

Look out for these boxes:

WHAT WOULD YOU DO?
Imagine what it would be like to make difficult choices in wartime.

REMEMBERING BRAVERY
Find out about the ways in which we remember courageous acts today.

NUMBER CRUNCHING
Learn the facts and figures about wars and battles.

SECRET HEROES
Find out about the brave individuals who didn't make it into the history books.

INTRODUCTION

Swaying in a wooden basket beneath a gas-filled balloon, Thaddeus Lowe stared down at the battlefield below. The American **Civil War** (1861–65) was fought between the **Union** and the **Confederate** states, and Lowe worked for the Union Army Balloon Corps. To report what he saw, he could send a telegraph message or drop a note over the side. When he wanted to land, he let some gas out of the balloon and was pulled down by a long rope.

It was a risky job. His balloon gave him a great view of his enemies, but it also gave them a great view of him. This made him an easy target for enemy gunfire.

From balloons to planes

When people first flew in hot air balloons in 1783, flying seemed like magic. For more than 100 years, balloons and airships (balloons with engines) were the only flying machines.

Then, in 1903, Wilbur and Orville Wright flew the world's first powered airplane. Within 12 years, pilots were battling in the skies.

▶ This is the *Intrepid*, one of Thaddeus Lowe's balloons.

Today's pilots

In the first decades of the 1900s, combat pilots flew at a speed of 220 kilometers (138 miles) per hour. Today, a fast-jet pilot in Afghanistan flies at over 1,600 kilometers (1,000 miles) per hour. The first pilots could feel the wind in their faces and the movement of the plane as they handled the controls. Modern jets, packed with computers and electronics, can almost fly themselves.

Pilots fly **fighter planes**, **bombers**, and helicopters. A pilot in danger has to make life or death decisions in just seconds.

▼ This U.S. Air Force pilot is ready for a high-speed mission over Afghanistan.

World War I took place from 1914 to 1918. It was fought between Germany and its supporters and the United Kingdom, France, Russia, and their supporters. The first air battles took place during this war. They were known as dogfights.

Twisting and turning in the air

The first combat planes had open **cockpits**. To keep warm at a height of 3,000 meters (10,000 feet), pilots wore thick coats and gloves. During a dogfight the planes twisted and turned, while machine guns shot out bullets. Some damaged planes managed to make a crash-landing. If a pilot was shot or his plane burst into flames, he was usually killed.

The Red Baron

The best, or luckiest, pilots became known as aces. The most famous ace was Manfred von Richthofen of Germany. Known as the Red Baron, because his plane was painted red, he shot down 80 enemy planes.

The Red Baron's luck ran out in April 1918. Flying a three-winged **triplane**, he followed a Sopwith Camel **biplane** flown by a Canadian pilot named Wilfrid May. It was May's first mission. As the Red Baron chased May, another Canadian named Roy Brown zoomed down behind the red German plane and fired his machine-gun. Australian soldiers also shot at the Red Baron as he flew low over the battlefield in Amiens, France.

The red plane crashed, and Richthofen was found dead in the wreck. The Canadian pilots lived to fight another day.

▶ When war broke out in 1914, Manfred von Richthofen (the Red Baron) was only 22. Most World War I pilots were very young.

6

NUMBER CRUNCHING

The Red Baron's Fokker triplane was light but slow. Its top speed was 165 kilometers (103 miles) per hour. It had two machine guns.

Zeppelin airships

Some pilots flew small planes, but others went up in huge airships. These were bigger than today's airplanes. Airships were gas-filled balloons with engines and **propellers**.

In 1915 German Zeppelin airships dropped bombs on the United Kingdom. This was the first time cities had been bombed from the air. Zeppelin LZ37 was 158 meters (518 feet) long, and it traveled through the air at 84 kilometers (52 miles) per hour. On June 7, 1915, it set off from Belgium to raid the United Kingdom.

Plane versus airship

British pilot Reginald Warneford was flying a French **fighter plane** when he saw the Zeppelin LZ37 approaching. He attacked by flying higher and dropping bombs on it. He wrote in his report that "there was an explosion which lifted my machine and turned it over." When his plane was flying straight again, he saw the airship falling in flames. Amazingly, Alfred Muhler, one of LZ37's crew, survived. He was in one of the cabins. The airship crashed through the roof of a convent (a religious home) and he landed on a bed, still alive.

Warneford had to land his plane in a field to make repairs, hoping the German soldiers would not catch him. Then he flew back to his base. He was killed 10 days later while flying. The tail fin of his plane broke off and hit the propeller, and he crashed.

REMEMBERING BRAVERY

For his brave deed, Reginald Warneford was awarded the Victoria Cross, the most important medal in the United Kingdom.

This painting shows the end of the battle between a plane and an airship.

WORLD WAR II PILOTS IN DANGER

World War II lasted from 1939 to 1945. Germany, Japan, Italy, and their supporters fought the United Kingdom, the United States, the **Soviet Union**, and their supporters. There were terrible battles all over the world, and millions of people died.

▼ These men are running to their planes during a World War II training exercise.

The Battle of Britain

It is late summer in 1940. Farmers in England look up to see planes making patterns in the blue sky. Some are British fighters, but most of the black dots are German planes. This battle in the air is the Battle of Britain.

In the Battle of Britain, British Royal Air Force pilots flew day after day. Young pilots who had just finished their training had to learn fast from older pilots, such as Douglas Bader. Bader had artificial legs, but he still managed to fly a Spitfire **fighter plane**. Pilots from other countries fought in the Battle of Britain, too, including the United States.

Bob Doe's battle

Bob Doe joined the battle on August 15, 1940. Only 20 years old, he did not think he was a good pilot. He hated flying upside-down! Yet, by October, he had shot down 14 German aircraft.

He lost many friends. Between August 15 and September 7, 12 of the 15 pilots in his **squadron** were killed. Despite these losses, Doe worried more about showing fear than being shot down. He survived the war, living until 2010.

REMEMBERING BRAVERY

Billy Fiske was an American who flew Britain's Hurricane fighters in the Battle of Britain. On August 16, 1940, he landed safely in Sussex, England, but his plane caught fire. He later died of his burns. Fiske is honored with a plaque in St. Paul's Cathedral, in London, England. The plaque calls him an "American citizen who died that England might live."

Women pilots

During World War II, women pilots in the United States and the United Kingdom flew new planes from factories to airfields, but they did not take part in battles. The United Kingdom's Amy Johnson made record flights in the 1930s and flew Royal Air Force planes until she died in a crash in 1941. In the United States, Jacqueline Cochran led the Women Airforce Service Pilots (WASPs). After the war, she flew jets and became known as "the fastest woman in the world."

The Night Witches

The Soviet Union was the only country in which women pilots took part in battle. In 1941 Marina Raskova led her team in attacks on German soldiers. They flew slow planes, with a top speed of only 150 kilometers (94 miles) per hour. This was actually an advantage. The planes were so slow that the fast German fighter planes found it hard to shoot at them.

Raskova and her pilots flew at night. They sneaked in just above trees and hedges, so the Germans soldiers could not see them. Another trick they used was to switch off their engines so that the Germans could not hear the planes glide in.

After they dropped the bombs, the pilots restarted their engines. Sometimes Raskova and her pilots made more than 10 attacks in one night. The Germans called them the Night Witches.

▲ Here you can see Marina Raskova (right) with two of her pilots.

SECRET HEROES

Women mechanics kept the Night Witches' planes flying, even in winter when ice covered the wings. In the United States and the United Kingdom, women factory workers built planes. Women also worked in air force control centers. They directed planes by radio.

▲ This member of the British Women's Auxiliary Air Force (WAAF) is talking to a pilot from the bomber command base.

Bombers and fighters

During World War II, the U.S. **bombers** that flew into enemy territory in Germany and Japan always had fighter planes flying alongside them. The fighter pilots' task was to protect their bombers from the enemy, while the bombers concentrated on the attack.

The Tuskegee airmen

In 1941 the first group of African-American fighter pilots began training for the war in Tuskegee, Alabama. They flew P-47 Thunderbolts and P-51 Mustang fighters with red tails.

A bomber pilot said, "The red tails were always out there, just where we wanted them." One famous Tuskegee airman was Lee Archer, who, on October 22, 1944, shot down three German planes in a single day.

On March 24, 1945, the red tails flew along with the bombers that were going to attack the city of Berlin, Germany. They saw the German Me-262s flying in to attack them. The Me-262 was faster than any other plane at the time. Even so, three Tuskegee airmen, named Roscoe Brown, Jr., Charles Brantley, and Earl Lane, each shot one down. This meant that the bombers could complete their mission over Berlin.

REMEMBERING BRAVERY

Some Tuskegee airmen were killed on their first mission and never got the chance to be heroes. But Lee Archer flew an amazing 169 missions. He served in the U.S. Air Force until 1970, and he died in 2010. Along with many others, he is remembered at the Tuskegee Airmen National Historic Site in Tuskegee, Alabama.

▼ These P-51 Mustang planes are similar to those flown by the Tuskegee airmen.

BOMBER CREWS IN ACTION

A World War II **bomber** mission could last many hours. The crew onboard included a pilot, a **navigator**, a bomb-aimer, a radio operator, and machine-gunners. Each man kept a lookout for enemy fighters. Danger could also come from **anti-aircraft guns** on the ground below. If a bomber plane was hit, it would try to fly home and crash-land.

If a bomber plane broke up or caught fire, the crew members had to use their parachutes and jump out. Often, crews watched their friends' planes crash to the ground far below. The next day, those who had made it back might have to go out on yet another mission.

How did fliers escape?

George Silva was a radio operator in a U.S. B-17 bomber plane. In March 1944 he and his crew, including the pilot Bob Cook and the gunner Dick Thayer, took off from England to bomb German airfields in France. While flying over enemy territory, their plane was hit by gunfire from the ground. The front end of the plane exploded, and part of its wing and one of its four engines fell off.

As the B-17 plunged to the ground, Silva and the others grabbed their parachutes. They jumped out of the plane and landed beside a German gun-crew. Silva, Cook, and Thayer were taken prisoner. Six of their crewmates died.

▶ These B-17 bombers are flying over Germany in 1943.

NUMBER CRUNCHING

The B-17, known as the Flying Fortress, had 13 machine guns. The British Lancaster had eight guns. Both these planes had a top speed of around 458 kilometers (285 miles) per hour and could fly for 3,200 kilometers (2,000 miles) while carrying bombs.

The Dambusters

A pilot in a Lancaster bomber plane flies at 18 meters (60 feet) above a lake, toward a wall of concrete. Underneath his plane is a can-shaped bomb. He must drop it at just the right moment, so that it skips across the water like a skimming stone—and blows up a dam!

What was the bouncing bomb?

In 1943 British Royal Air Force pilots of the 617 **Squadron** were trained to drop "bouncing bombs." What were they for? Inventor Barnes Wallis and bomber pilot Guy Gibson were among the few who knew the answer. They were going to target German dams and smash them, so the water would flood nearby factories. Gibson told his men the whole story on the afternoon of May 16, 1943. That night they flew to Germany.

▼ Dambuster crew members are boarding their Lancaster bomber.

Attack on the dams

Gibson led the attack on the Moehne Dam in Germany. After blasting a hole in the dam, Gibson led a second attack, this time on the Eder Dam. A third dam, the Sorpe, was also attacked. Only 11 of 19 bombers came home, and the Germans mended the dams. However, the bravery and daring of the Dambusters helped keep up the spirits of the **Allies**. In 1955 the story was made into a movie called *The Dambusters*.

REMEMBERING BRAVERY

Guy Gibson was killed in 1944. His plane crashed in Steenbergen, Holland. In honor of their brave actions, streets in the town were later named after Gibson and his navigator, Jim Warwick.

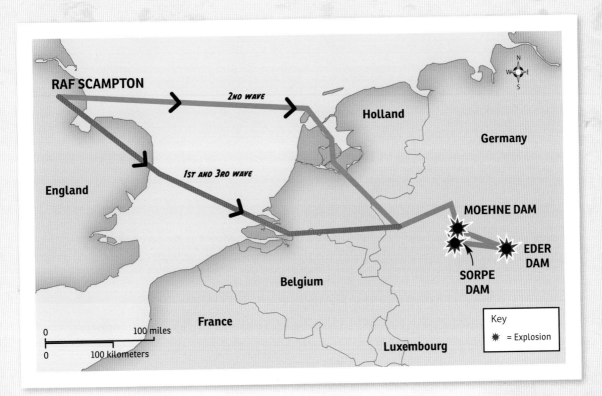

▲ The Dambusters flew from the Royal Air Force base at Scampton, England, in three groups, or waves. Their targets were the Moehne, Eder, and Sorpe dams in Germany.

Giant bombers over Japan

In 1944 U.S. pilots began flying the giant B-29 Superfortress. This new bomber could fly for 8,000 kilometers (5,000 miles). It could also fly so high that no fighter could follow it.

Two B-29s made history in 1945, when they dropped the first **atomic bombs** on two cities in Japan. These attacks forced Japan to surrender, bringing an end to World War II.

Who dropped the first atomic bomb?

Colonel Paul W. Tibbets, Jr., was a skilled bomber pilot who had flown B-17s in Europe. In 1945 Tibbets was given secret orders to train a special team of pilots in Utah. Flying B-29s, they practiced dropping a new secret weapon. There were rumors that this weapon was a bomb that could destroy a city.

Enola Gay

On August 6, 1945, Tibbets and his crew took off from the Mariana Islands, in the Pacific Ocean. He flew a bomber called *Enola Gay,* which was named after his mother. The bomb-aimer Major Thomas Ferebee released the bomb over the city of Hiroshima.

Tibbets made a sharp turn, but even at 9,400 meters (31,000 feet), the blast shook the B-29. Tibbets felt his teeth tingle. The explosion sent a mushroom-shaped cloud rising high above the plane, as Tibbets flew away at top speed.

How the bombs ended the war

The bomb killed more than 70,000 people in Hiroshima. More people died later from the effects of atomic **radiation**. On August 9, 1945, a second B-29, piloted by Charles W. Sweeney, dropped a second atomic bomb over the city of Nagasaki. Realizing there was no defense against such bombs, the Japanese stopped fighting. The war was over.

▲ This is the crew of *Enola Gay.* They dropped the
first atomic bomb on the city of Hiroshima, in Japan.

Imagine that you are flying a plane over the desert, at only 15 meters (50 feet) above the sand. Suddenly, all you can see are orange flames and black smoke. Your plane has been hit by a missile! This happened to two British pilots during the Gulf War in 1991.

The Gulf War began when Iraq attacked Kuwait, a neighboring country. A **United Nations (UN)** force went in to stop Iraq. UN planes took off from bases in the desert.

On January 17, 1991, pilot John Peters and **navigator** John Nichol took off in a Tornado jet on their first mission, to bomb an airfield. After taking on fuel from a flying tanker, they flew in very low. But an Iraqi missile streaked in, and the Tornado became a fireball.

▶ This is John Peters (front) and John Nichol in their Tornado jet.

Eject!

The men pulled the **ejector seat** levers. They were thrown clear of the plane just seconds before it hit the ground. They landed using parachutes. Then they buried the equipment they would not need, such as their life jackets. Nichol also ate his map, to destroy any secret information! They were captured by Iraqi soldiers and held in prison for 47 days. They were treated badly, but after their release they went home and were both soon flying again.

WHAT WOULD YOU DO?

A rocket hits you. Do you try to fly on, land, or eject? Remember, pilots have only seconds in which to make decisions.

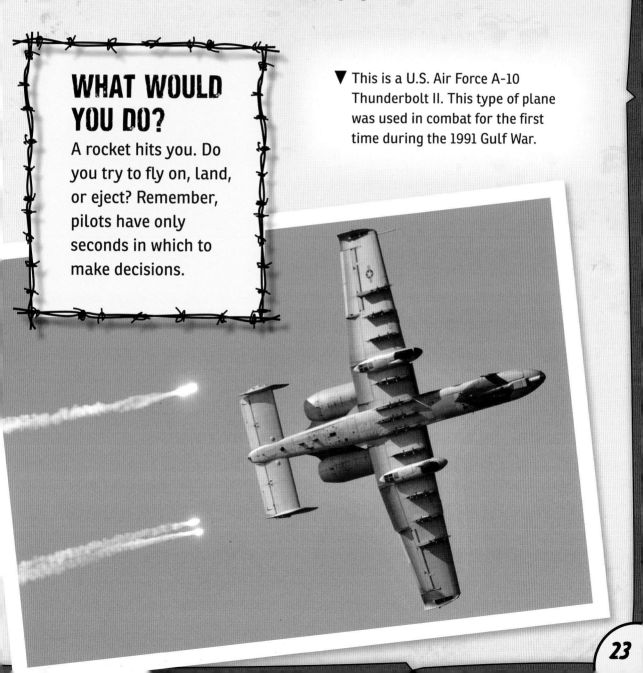

▼ This is a U.S. Air Force A-10 Thunderbolt II. This type of plane was used in combat for the first time during the 1991 Gulf War.

Helicopters in Afghanistan

Helicopters can land almost anywhere, but they are slower than winged airplanes, so they are easier to shoot down.

Hundreds of U.S. and **NATO** helicopters fly every day in the war against the **Taliban** in Afghanistan. There are hardly any roads in the far-off areas where the war is fought, so helicopters are often the easiest way to get around. The Taliban have no pilots or planes, but they do have hand-held missiles and roadside bombs. Helicopter pilots risk their lives every day.

NUMBER CRUNCHING

Black Hawk helicopters weigh almost 4 tons and carry two machine guns.

▼ An injured soldier is being helped into a Black Hawk helicopter on a medical evacuation mission.

How do helicopters rescue people?

The U.S. Army's **medical evacuation** (Medevac) pilots fly helicopters around Afghanistan to rescue wounded soldiers. It can often be very dangerous work.

On April 2, 2010, a patrol of German soldiers was taken by surprise by Taliban fighters near the city of Kunduz. Eleven soldiers were injured. Black Hawk helicopters flew in to rescue the injured men.

Pilot Jason LaCrosse flew one of the helicopters. His aircraft was shot at by the Taliban as he tried to land, so he had to circle before dropping down to pick up two of the German soldiers. The helicopter rushed them to a hospital, then flew back to help rescue the other soldiers.

REMEMBERING BRAVERY

For their bravery, Jason Lacrosse and 13 other Black Hawk crew members received Germany's Gold Cross medal. They were the first non-Germans to be given this honor. Crew member Antonio Gattis explained that all NATO soldiers in Afghanistan were "like family," so "we just went out there and did what we had to do."

CONCLUSION

Today, pilots fly planes that use some amazing technology. Wars can even be fought without pilots in planes, using **drones**. Drones are planes flown using computers and video technology. Someone sitting at a desk in the United States can fly a drone around the mountains of Afghanistan, thousands of miles away.

Yet, even with such incredible weaponry, all air forces need their pilots—men and women who are fit, well trained, and disciplined.

Women at war

Women pilots fly in combat **squadrons** and in demonstration squadrons. Demonstration squadrons perform in air shows, at fairs, and for special occasions.

In 1998 Lieutenant Kendra Williams became the first U.S. woman pilot to take part in a battle. She flew a F/A-18 jet over Iraq.

In 2010 Kirsty Moore joined the United Kingdom's famous demonstration squadron, the Red Arrows, and became the first female demonstration pilot.

Latifa Nabizada is the first and, so far, the only woman pilot in the Afghan Air Corps. Hina Tahir is a fighter pilot in the Pakistan Air Force. All these women are helping to inspire a new generation of pilots and soldiers.

What makes a good pilot?

Pilots in World War I flew planes made from wood and cloth. A pilot had to be brave just to take off in such flimsy machines. Modern pilots can fly faster than sound. Events happen very fast all around them, so they need to be able to react quickly. Flying a supersonic jet is a bit like being on an amusement park ride at 10 times the normal speed, while playing a computer game! A good pilot must stay calm and alert. Danger can be just behind the next cloud.

A drone is launched
from a German base in
Kunduz, Afghanistan.

UNITED STATES
In the skies over the United States, daring balloon pilots looked down on the enemy during the American **Civil War**.

EUROPE
During World War I and World War II, pilots fought air battles over Europe.

UNITED KINGDOM
During World War II, brave pilots won the Battle of Britain in 1940, saving the United Kingdom from invasion.

SOVIET UNION
Soviet women pilots fought the Germans during World War II. They were known as the "Night Witches."

JAPAN
B-29 planes dropped **atomic bombs** on Japan, ending World War II.

IRAQ
John Peters and John Nichol are taken prisoner during the Gulf War.

AFGHANISTAN
U.S. Army helicopters rescue soldiers wounded in the war against the **Taliban**.

GLOSSARY

Allies nations fighting together during World War II, including the United States and the United Kingdom

anti-aircraft gun gun on the ground that fires at planes high above

atomic bomb very powerful bomb that is made using nuclear power

biplane plane with two sets of wings fixed one above the other

bomber plane made to fly long distances and drop bombs on the enemy

civil war war between different groups of people in the same country

cockpit name for the pilot's seat and control area inside a plane

Confederate one of the southern U.S. states that, in the 1800s, wanted to break away and form their own government

drone robot plane controlled from the ground, without a pilot onboard

ejector seat system that launches a pilot out of a crashing plane

fighter plane plane built to move quickly and easily, so that it can fight and shoot down other planes

medical evacuation taking wounded people to places where they can be treated safely

NATO (North Atlantic Treaty Organization) group of 28 nations that have agreed to defend each other in the event of attack

navigator person whose job is to keep a plane flying to the right places

propellor shaft with revolving blades that drives a plane forward

radiation energy that can harm or kill people if they are exposed to it

Soviet Union communist state made up of Russia and several neighboring countries, which existed between 1922 and 1991

squadron group of pilots who live and fly together, including their ground crews

Taliban group who ruled Afghanistan until removed from power in 2001. Members of the Taliban continue to fight in Afghanistan.

triplane plane with three sets of wings fixed one above the other

Union group of northern U.S. states that fought against the southern states that tried to set up their own government in the 1800s

United Nations (UN) international organization representing nearly all of the world's countries

FIND OUT MORE

Books

Graham, Ian. *You Wouldn't Want to Be a World War II Pilot!: Air Battles You Might Not Survive*. New York: Franklin Watts, 2010.

Orr, Tamra. *What's So Great About the Tuskegee Airmen*? Hockessin, Del.: Mitchell Lane, 2010.

Williams, Brian. *World at War—World War II: Life as a Fighter Pilot*. Chicago: Heinemann Library, 2006.

Websites

www.nationalmuseum.af.mil/
Learn more about the history of war planes on this website of the National Museum of the U.S. Air Force.

www.pbs.org/greatwar/
This PBS website offers lots of information about World War I, including helpful features like maps and timelines.

www.history.com/interactives/wwii-experience
This History Channel website has lots of information and interactive features to help you learn more about World War II.

Places to visit

National Museum of the U.S. Air Force
1100 Spaatz Street
Wright-Patterson AFB, Ohio 45433
www.nationalmuseum.af.mil

Smithsonian National Air and Space Museum
Independence Ave at 6th Street, SW
Washington, D.C. 20560
www.nasm.si.edu

Visit the National Museum of the U.S. Air Force and the Smithsonian National Air and Space Museum to learn more about the wars and planes discussed in this book.

INDEX